HUMAN PSYCHOLOGY MEETS INTELLIGENT AUTOMATION

THE BRAINF*CKING GUIDE FOR BUILDING RELATIONS

-Gurnain Singh Wadhwa

HUMAN PSYCHOLOGY MEETS INTELLIGENT AUTOMATION

About the Author

Gurnain Singh Wadhwa is an excellent engineering undergraduate with a passion for innovation and problem-solving. With a diverse background in engineering, he has successfully completed numerous research projects, developed cutting-edge technology, and implemented innovative solutions that have positively impacted people's lives.

In addition to his work in the field of engineering, Gurnain is also an accomplished author. His first book, "Human Psychology meets Intelligent automation: The brainf*cking guide for building relations is a testament to his creativity, critical thinking skills, and his ability to bridge the gap between technology and humanity. In his book, Gurnain draws from his extensive experience in engineering and his interest in human psychology to explore the intersection of these two fields. He offers insights and perspectives on how AI can be harnessed to improve human well-being and enhance our overall quality of life.

As a thought leader in the field of engineering and technology, Gurnain has been invited to speak at numerous conferences and events. He is a regular contributor to industry publications and has been recognized for his contributions to the field of engineering.

When he is not working on new projects or writing, Gurnain enjoys spending time with his family and exploring new technologies and ideas.

SCAN QR TO KNOW MORE

Dedication

To my cat, who I suspect only kept me around for the warm laptop keyboard to lay on. Your frequent naps on my workspace were a constant source of frustration and amusement, but I would not have it any other way. You are my muse, my inspiration, and my forever feline companion.

Table of Contents

- Proper email communication: addressing, tone, and structure
- Understanding tone in text-based communication
- The importance of grammar and spelling in digital communication
- Effective use of social media for professional communication
- Handling communication in group chats: including everyone and staying on topic
- Using appropriate language in digital communication
- Responding to messages in a timely manner
- Handling conflicts and misunderstandings in digital communication
- Respecting others' privacy and boundaries in digital communication

5) Special AI Tool

6) Conspiracy Theories (Tackling Conspiracies)

- Workplace conspiracy
- Relationship conspiracy
- Family conspiracy
- Romantic conspiracy
- Academic conspiracy

INTRODUCTION

Are you tired of feeling like you're in a one-sided relationship with your technology? Do you long for the days when your biggest problem was figuring out how to program your VCR? Well, fear not my friends, because I've got the ultimate guide for building relationships with the technology of today.

In my book, "HUMAN PSYCHOLOGY MEETS INTELLIGENT AUTOMATION: The Brainf*cking guide for building relations" I'll teach you how to create meaningful connections with your friends, family, partner, etc. We'll explore the world of artificial intelligence and how it intersects with our very human need for connection and understanding. And, of course, we'll do it all with a healthy dose of humor and wit.

So, buckle up, folks. It's time to take your relationship with technology to the next level. Just don't be surprised even if your virtual assistant starts asking you out on a date.

PART 1

Introduction to Human Psychology and AI

HUMAN PSYCHOLOGY

Human psychology is the scientific study of human behavior and mental processes. It aims to understand the complexities of human behavior, including how we think, feel, and act, and the factors that influence these processes. The field of psychology has a long and rich history, dating back to ancient Greece and Rome, where philosophers such as Plato and Aristotle pondered the nature of the mind and human behavior. However, it wasn't until the late 19th century that psychology emerged as a scientific discipline.

The father of modern psychology is widely regarded as Wilhelm Wundt, who founded the first experimental psychology laboratory in Leipzig, Germany, in 1879. Wundt believed that the study of human psychology should be based on empirical observation and scientific experimentation, rather than speculation and philosophical musings. This approach marked the beginning of psychology as a scientific discipline, and it has since evolved into a vast and multi-disciplinary field that encompasses many different areas of focus.

Cognitive Psychology:

One of the most influential areas of psychology is cognitive psychology, which focuses on the mental processes involved in thinking, perceiving, and remembering. Cognitive psychology seeks to understand how people acquire, process, and use information from the world around them. For example, cognitive psychologists study how we perceive the visual world, how we learn language, and how we solve problems.

Developmental Psychology:

Another important area of psychology is developmental psychology, which is concerned with how people change and develop over their lifespan, from infancy to old age. Developmental psychologists' study physical, cognitive, and social changes that occur over time, and how these changes are influenced by genetics, environment, and culture. For example, developmental psychologists study how infants develop attachment to their caregivers, how children acquire language, and how aging affects cognitive function.

Clinical Psychology:

Clinical psychology is a branch of psychology that is concerned with the diagnosis, treatment, and prevention of mental health disorders. Clinical psychologists work with individuals, families, and groups to help people cope with a wide range of psychological and emotional issues. They use a variety of therapeutic techniques, including talk therapy, behavior modification, and medication, to help people improve their mental health.

Social Psychology:

Social psychology is the study of how people interact with each other in social settings. Social psychologists study topics such as group dynamics, social influence, and interpersonal relationships. They are interested in understanding how people perceive and interpret social situations, how social norms and expectations influence behavior, and how people form and maintain relationships.

Personality Psychology:

Personality psychology is the study of the patterns of thoughts, feelings, and behaviors that make each person unique. Personality psychologists study traits, such as extraversion, agreeableness, and conscientiousness, and how these traits influence behavior. They are interested in understanding how personality develops over time and how it is influenced by genetics, environment, and culture.

Applications of Psychology:

The study of human psychology has many practical applications in a variety of fields. For example, psychologists use their knowledge of human behavior and mental processes to help people live happier, healthier, and more productive lives. Psychologists work in fields such as education, health care, business, sports, and the arts, applying their knowledge to improve performance, enhance learning, and promote well-being

Psychology as a field of study seeks to understand the intricacies of human behavior and mental processes. It encompasses a wide range of topics, from basic cognitive processes such as perception and attention, to complex social behaviors like communication and cooperation. It also includes the study of abnormal behavior, mental disorders, and treatments for psychological issues.

The study of human psychology can be traced back to ancient civilizations like the Greeks and the Egyptians, who were interested in understanding human behavior and thought processes. However, psychology as a modern scientific discipline began in the late 19th century with the work of pioneers such as Wilhelm Wundt, who is often referred to as the "father of psychology."

Since then, the field of psychology has continued to evolve and expand, with new subfields and areas of focus emerging over time. Today, psychology is a broad and diverse field that encompasses numerous approaches and theories, including cognitive psychology, behavioral psychology, social psychology, developmental psychology, and more.

One of the key features of psychology is its interdisciplinary nature. It draws on insights and research from other fields such as neuroscience, biology, sociology, and anthropology to better understand human behavior and mental processes. Psychology also has practical applications in areas like mental health, education, business, and public policy.

Overall, the study of human psychology is a fascinating and complex field with much to discover and explore. It offers insights into what makes us human, how we interact with each other and the world around us, and how we can improve our lives and relationships. In this book, we will explore the intersection of psychology and AI, and how these two fields are shaping our understanding of ourselves and our world.

ARTIFICIAL INTELLIGENCE

Artificial intelligence (AI) is a rapidly growing field that seeks to create machines or computer programs that can perform tasks that would normally require human intelligence to complete. The goal of AI is to create machines that can learn, reason, and make decisions on their own, without the need for human intervention.

AI has a long and fascinating history, dating back to the 1950s. Early researchers in the field were optimistic about the potential for machines to perform complex tasks that were previously thought to be impossible for non-human entities. However, progress in the field was slow, and it wasn't until the 1980s that AI began to gain traction and show promising results.

Today, AI is used in a wide range of applications, from self-driving cars to virtual personal assistants like Siri and Alexa. It is also used in industries like healthcare, finance, and manufacturing, where it can help to automate repetitive tasks and improve efficiency.

There are many different approaches to AI, each with its own strengths and weaknesses. Some of the most common approaches include machine learning, deep learning, and natural language processing. Machine learning involves training a computer program to recognize patterns and make decisions based on those patterns. Deep learning is a subset of machine learning that involves training a neural network to recognize complex patterns. Natural language processing involves teaching computers to understand and interpret human language.

While AI has the potential to revolutionize many aspects of our lives, there are also concerns about its impact on society. Some worry that AI could lead to widespread job loss, while others are concerned about the ethical implications of creating machines that can make decisions on their own.

Overall, AI is a fascinating and rapidly evolving field with many exciting possibilities. As we continue to develop and refine this technology, it will be important to consider its potential impact on society and work to ensure that it is used in a responsible and ethical manner.

HUMAN PSYCHOLOGY MEETS INTELLIGENT AUTOMATION

The impact of AI on human psychology is a complex and multifaceted issue. On one hand, AI has the potential to enhance our cognitive abilities and improve our mental health by providing access to personalized therapy and counseling. On the other hand, the increasing reliance on AI for social interaction and decision-making could have negative consequences for our ability to form meaningful connections with others and make independent choices. It is important to explore both the positive and negative impacts of AI on human psychology in order to fully understand its potential implications for society. In this book you will learn how to use AI smarty for building connections or relations.

NOTE

BRAINF*CK WILL START
FROM HERE

PART 2

Strategies for Building Meaningful Connections in the Age of AI

BUILDING AND MAINTAINING CONNECTIONS WITH FRIENDS AND FAMILY

Building and maintaining connections with friends and family is a critical aspect of human psychology that has been studied extensively over the years. It is a fundamental human need to feel connected and supported by others, and research has shown that strong social connections are linked to numerous benefits, such as improved physical and mental health, increased happiness, and greater resilience to stress and adversity.

There are several ways to build and maintain meaningful connections with friends and family. One important factor is to prioritize face-to-face interactions whenever possible. While technology can be useful for staying in touch with loved ones who are far away, there is no substitute for real-life interactions. Spending quality time together, engaging in shared activities, and having meaningful conversations can help strengthen the bond between individuals.

Another key strategy is to be intentional about limiting the use of technology during social gatherings. In today's digital age, it is easy to get distracted by phones, laptops, and other devices, which can take away from the experience of being present and fully engaged with others. Creating technology-free zones or times during social gatherings can help people connect on a deeper level and foster more meaningful relationships.

It's also essential to communicate effectively and openly with friends and family members. Being a good listener, showing empathy and understanding, and expressing gratitude for the people in our lives can help build trust and strengthen relationships. Additionally, it's crucial to prioritize quality over quantity when it comes to social connections. Having a small circle of close, supportive friends and family members can be more valuable than a large network of acquaintances.

Building and maintaining connections with friends and family is a complex process that involves several psychological aspects. For instance, the quality of our relationships is influenced by our ability to regulate emotions, express ourselves authentically, and communicate effectively. It is also important to understand that relationships go through natural ups and downs, and that conflict is a normal part of any human interaction. Being able to navigate conflict constructively and repair relationships when needed is crucial for maintaining long-term connections.

In addition to the psychological aspects, social factors such as culture, gender, and socioeconomic status can also impact the quality of our relationships. For example, individuals from collectivistic cultures may prioritize family and community relationships over individual autonomy, while those from individualistic cultures may prioritize personal achievement and independence. Gender and socioeconomic status can also influence the types of social connections people have and the support they receive from others.

In addition to the factors mentioned previously, there are several other aspects that play a role in building and maintaining connections with friends and family. One of these is the concept of reciprocity, which refers to the mutual exchange of support and resources in a relationship. This can include emotional support, practical assistance, and social opportunities.

Another important aspect is the concept of trust, which is built over time through consistent behavior and communication. Trust involves a belief that the other person has our best interests at heart and will act in a trustworthy manner. Trust is crucial for building deep connections, as it allows us to be vulnerable and share our thoughts, feelings, and experiences without fear of judgement or betrayal.

Building and maintaining connections with friends and family can also be influenced by external factors such as life transitions, geographic distance, and social norms. For example, moving to a new city or starting a new job can impact our social networks, while cultural or societal norms may influence the types of relationships that are valued and prioritized.

Overall, building and maintaining meaningful connections with friends and family is a multifaceted process that involves both psychological and social factors. It requires intentionality, effort, and a willingness to navigate conflict and repair relationships when needed. By prioritizing face-to-face interactions, limiting technology use, communicating effectively, and understanding the various factors that impact our relationships, we can cultivate strong, supportive connections that enrich our lives.

ROLE OF AI IN BUILDING AND MAINTAINING CONNECTIONS WITH FRIENDS AND FAMILY

When it comes to building connections with new people, AI can be a valuable tool. For example, social media platforms that utilize AI algorithms can help you find people with similar interests as you and the person you've just met, giving you common ground to start a conversation and build a friendship. AI-powered language translation tools can also be useful if you and the person you've met speak different languages, allowing you to communicate more easily and break down language barriers. Additionally, AI-powered recommendation systems can suggest activities or events that you and the person might enjoy attending together, helping to facilitate deeper connections. However, it's important to remember that while AI can be helpful in making new connections, it's ultimately up to you to put in the effort to build and maintain those relationships over time. AI can't replace the importance of genuine human interaction and connection.

Use cases of AI in building Connection

The author of this book has also developed a cutting-edge chatbot that can assist individuals in improving their communication skills. This chatbot is trained to simulate different communication styles, including gender, age, marital status, occupation, and personality traits, to provide users with a highly personalized experience. For instance, if someone is interested in improving their business communication skills, they can simply adjust the chatbot's characteristics accordingly and receive tailored feedback on their performance. To access this exclusive tool, individuals can reach out to the author through LinkedIn and take their first step towards becoming a more effective communicator.

Another Case is, let's say you meet a new girl in your classroom who speaks a different language than you. In this situation, you can use AI-powered language translation tools like Google Translate to communicate with her. For example, if she speaks

Spanish and you only know English, you can use the translation tool to convert your messages into Spanish and vice versa.

To implement this, you can simply download the Google Translate app on your phone and use the camera feature to translate text in real-time. You can also use the audio feature to translate spoken language in real-time. So, when you meet the new girl, you can use the app to translate your messages and have a conversation with her in real-time, even if you don't know her language.

This use case can help to build a meaningful connection with someone who you otherwise wouldn't be able to communicate with due to a language barrier. By using AI-powered translation tools, you can show that you're willing to make an effort to understand and communicate with the other person, which can help to establish a bond and build a stronger relationship.

NAVIGATING THE WORLD OF DATING

Navigating the world of dating can be challenging, especially when it comes to communication. Effective communication skills are essential in building and maintaining romantic relationships. Being able to express oneself clearly and listen actively to one's partner is crucial for a healthy relationship.

One important communication skill in dating is active listening. It involves not only hearing what the other person is saying but also understanding their point of view. When you actively listen to your partner, you show them that you care about their thoughts and feelings. This can help to build trust and establish a strong emotional connection.

Another important aspect of communication in dating is expressing oneself clearly and assertively. It involves being honest and open about one's thoughts, feelings, and expectations in a relationship. By communicating clearly and assertively, both partners can avoid misunderstandings and conflicts.

Effective communication in dating also involves being able to read and interpret nonverbal cues such as body language and tone of voice. Understanding these cues can help to better understand your partner's emotions and intentions.

Finally, it's important to remember that dating is a two-way street, and that successful relationships are built on mutual respect and trust. This means being honest and transparent about your intentions and expectations, and being willing to work through any conflicts or challenges that arise along the way.

To help individuals improve their communication skills in dating, the author has developed a chatbot that can be customized to meet specific needs. By setting the chatbot's gender, personality traits, and other characteristics, the user can practice and improve their communication skills in a safe and controlled environment. This can be accessed by contacting the author through LinkedIn.

Overall, by focusing on developing strong communication skills, positive behaviors and attitudes, and mutual respect and trust, you can navigate the world of dating with confidence and ease.

USE OF AI IN DATING

The use of AI in dating for an individual person can be incredibly useful. One way is through the use of AI-powered dating apps that use algorithms to match individuals based on their interests, preferences, and behavior. These apps can also use machine learning to constantly improve their matching algorithms and suggest better matches over time. Another way AI can be used is through the analysis of online dating profiles and conversations to identify patterns that lead to successful matches. AI-powered chatbots can also be used to help individuals improve their communication skills and practice interacting with potential partners. Additionally, AI can be used to detect and remove fake profiles or scammers, making online dating safer and more trustworthy. Overall, AI can help individuals navigate the world of dating by providing personalized recommendations, improving communication skills, and increasing safety.

BUILDING PROFESSIONAL NETWORKS

Building a professional network is crucial for success in any career, and psychology can play a significant role in this process. One of the fundamental aspects of networking is building relationships with people, and psychology can help you understand how to form and maintain these relationships.

Firstly, it's important to understand that people have different personalities, communication styles, and needs. Psychology can provide insights into these differences and help you tailor your approach to connect with different individuals. For example, if you're trying to network with someone who is introverted, you may need to use different communication strategies than you would with an extroverted individual.

Furthermore, understanding body language and nonverbal communication can help you build rapport with others. Being able to read and respond appropriately to nonverbal cues can help establish trust and build relationships. Additionally, developing emotional intelligence can help you navigate tricky interpersonal situations and build stronger relationships.

Networking events and conferences can be overwhelming for some people. Understanding how to manage anxiety and stress can help you stay calm and present yourself confidently. Additionally, developing active listening skills can help you engage in meaningful conversations and make a strong impression.

Finally, maintaining relationships is key to building a successful professional network. Psychology can help you understand how to cultivate long-term relationships by being empathetic, supportive, and responsive to the needs of others. Regular check-ins and meaningful interactions can help ensure that your relationships remain strong and valuable over time.

In conclusion, psychology plays a critical role in building a successful professional network. By understanding personality types, communication styles, nonverbal cues, emotional intelligence, and relationship maintenance, you can form strong connections with others and advance your career.

Some additional points to consider when it comes to the role of psychology in building a professional network:

1. Self-awareness: Developing self-awareness is critical to building strong professional relationships. Knowing your own strengths, weaknesses, and communication style can help you navigate different personalities and build stronger connections. Understanding your own values, motivations, and interests can also help you find like-minded professionals and develop common ground.

2. Active listening: Being a good listener is key to building strong relationships, both personally and professionally. Active listening involves not just hearing what the other person is saying, but also understanding their perspective and responding appropriately. This can help you build trust and respect with colleagues, clients, and other professionals.

3. Emotional intelligence: Emotional intelligence refers to the ability to recognize and manage your own emotions, as well as the emotions of others. In a professional context, emotional intelligence can help you navigate conflict, manage stress, and build strong relationships. This can include skills like empathy, self-awareness, and effective communication.

4. Networking strategies: There are a variety of strategies you can use to build your professional network, depending on your goals and interests. Some common approaches include attending networking events, joining industry associations or online communities, seeking out mentors or advisors, and leveraging social media platforms like LinkedIn.

5. Building trust: Building trust is critical to building strong professional relationships. This can involve being reliable, following through on commitments, and maintaining confidentiality when appropriate. It can also involve being open and honest in your communication, even when it may be uncomfortable.

By understanding and applying principles of psychology to building your professional network, you can develop stronger relationships, build your reputation, and advance your career.

USE OF AI IN BUILDING PROFESSIONAL NETWORK

An individual person can use AI in building their professional network in a variety of ways. One approach is to use AI-powered networking tools to help identify and connect with people who have similar interests or backgrounds. These tools can analyze your online activity and suggest relevant contacts and groups to join.

Another way to use AI is to leverage personalized communication. AI-powered chatbots can be used to initiate conversations with potential professional contacts. By incorporating natural language processing and machine learning, chatbots can learn from previous conversations and personalize their messaging to create a more engaging and effective interaction.

Additionally, AI-powered scheduling tools can help individuals manage their time more efficiently and schedule meetings with potential contacts. These tools can analyze availability and preferences to suggest optimal meeting times, reducing the need for back-and-forth communication.

Finally, AI can be used to analyze data and gain insights into your professional network. By tracking engagement metrics, such as email response rates and social media interactions, individuals can gain a better understanding of who is most engaged in their network and focus their efforts accordingly.

DEVELOPING EMPATHY AND EMOTIONAL INTELLIGENCE

Empathy and emotional intelligence are critical skills for building meaningful relationships and succeeding in both personal and professional settings. Empathy involves the ability to understand and share the feelings of others, while emotional intelligence encompasses the ability to recognize, understand, and manage one's own emotions, as well as those of others.

Developing empathy and emotional intelligence can be challenging, but there are several strategies that can help. One of the most important steps is to practice active listening. This means focusing fully on what the other person is saying, without distractions, and reflecting back what they have said to ensure you have understood their perspective.

Another strategy is to practice mindfulness and self-reflection. This involves taking time to be aware of your own emotions and reactions, and understanding how they might be affecting your interactions with others. Mindfulness can also help you to be more present and attentive in your relationships.

It's also important to recognize and manage your own emotions. This means being able to identify your emotions and understand how they impact your behavior and relationships. For example, if you are feeling anxious, you may be more likely to avoid social situations, which can negatively impact your ability to build and maintain relationships.

Developing empathy and emotional intelligence can have numerous benefits in both personal and professional settings. In personal relationships, these skills can lead to stronger connections, increased trust, and better communication. In professional settings, they can help you to collaborate more effectively with others, build stronger teams, and be a more effective leader.

Overall, developing empathy and emotional intelligence requires practice and patience, but the benefits are well worth the effort. By cultivating these skills, you can improve your relationships and achieve greater success in all areas of your life.

THE ROLE OF AI IN SHAPING HUMAN PSYCHOLOGY

Artificial intelligence (AI) is a rapidly advancing technology that is changing the way we interact with the world around us. As AI becomes more prevalent in our lives, it is also having a profound impact on human psychology. AI technologies are shaping the way we think, process information, and make decisions. In this article, we will explore the role of AI in shaping human psychology and the potential implications of this emerging trend.

One of the most significant ways in which AI is shaping human psychology is by changing the way we process information. AI technologies are capable of processing vast amounts of data and presenting it in a way that is easily understandable to humans. This ability is transforming the way we learn, making it easier and more efficient to absorb and process information. As a result, we are becoming more reliant on AI to help us navigate the world around us.

However, there is also concern that this reliance on AI could be having a negative impact on our cognitive abilities. As we become more reliant on AI to process information for us, we may be losing our ability to think critically and solve problems on our own. This could have serious implications for our ability to make decisions and navigate complex situations.

Another way in which AI is shaping human psychology is by changing the way we make decisions. AI technologies are capable of analyzing vast amounts of data and providing us with insights and recommendations that can help us make more informed decisions. This is particularly true in areas like finance, healthcare, and business, where AI is already being used to make complex decisions that were previously made by humans.

However, there is also concern that this reliance on AI to make decisions for us could be having a negative impact on our decision-making abilities. If we become too reliant on AI to make decisions for us, we may be losing our ability to think critically and evaluate information on our own. This could lead to a loss of autonomy and a decreased ability to make independent decisions.

Overall, the impact of AI on human psychology is a complex and evolving issue. While AI has the potential to revolutionize the way we process information and make decisions, there are also concerns about the potential negative impact on our cognitive abilities and decision-making processes. As AI continues to advance, it will be important for researchers and policymakers to closely monitor its impact on human psychology and take steps to mitigate any potential negative effects.

OVERCOMING AI-INDUCED SOCIAL ANXIETY

In the era of technology, we are constantly connected to our digital devices, which has given rise to a new form of anxiety known as "AI-Induced Social Anxiety." AI or Artificial Intelligence has revolutionized the way we interact with technology, making it easier and more accessible than ever before. However, as with any new technology, there are also potential downsides, one of which is the potential for AI to cause social anxiety and isolation. In this chapter, we will explore the impact of AI on social anxiety and provide tips for overcoming these challenges and building meaningful connections in social situations.

Impact of AI on Social Anxiety:

AI has the potential to cause social anxiety and isolation in a number of ways. Firstly, the constant availability of technology means that we are always connected, and this can create a sense of pressure to always be available and responsive. This can lead to feelings of social anxiety and a fear of missing out (FOMO) on important events or conversations. Secondly, AI can contribute to feelings of social isolation by providing an alternative to human interaction. For example, virtual assistants like Siri or Alexa can provide entertainment, information, and even emotional support, without the need for human interaction. While this may seem convenient, it can also lead to a sense of disconnection from the real world and other people.

Tips for Overcoming AI-Induced Social Anxiety:

Fortunately, there are several ways to overcome AI-induced social anxiety and build meaningful connections in social situations. Here are some tips:

Practice Mindfulness: Mindfulness involves being present in the moment and focusing on your thoughts and feelings without judgment. This can help you to become more aware of the impact that AI is having on your social interactions and to identify any negative thought patterns or behaviors that may be contributing to social anxiety.

Limit Your Use of Technology: Setting boundaries around your use of technology can help to reduce feelings of social anxiety and isolation. For example, you could try turning off notifications during social events or limiting your use of social media to specific times of day.

Seek Out Meaningful Interactions: While AI can be convenient, it cannot replace the value of human interaction. Seek out meaningful interactions with others, whether it be through joining a club, attending a social event, or volunteering in your community.

Practice Self-Compassion: Social anxiety can be difficult to overcome, but it is important to be kind to yourself throughout the process. Remember that everyone experiences social anxiety at some point in their lives, and that it is a normal human emotion.

Seek Professional Help: If social anxiety is impacting your daily life, it may be helpful to seek professional help. A therapist can provide support and guidance in managing social anxiety and building meaningful connections.

In conclusion, AI has the potential to contribute to social anxiety and isolation, but it is important to remember that we are ultimately in control of how we interact with technology. By practicing mindfulness, setting boundaries around technology use, seeking out meaningful interactions, practicing self-compassion, and seeking professional help when needed, we can overcome AI-induced social anxiety and build meaningful connections in social situations.

OVERCOMING RELATIONS INDUCED ANXIETY

Social anxiety is a common issue faced by many individuals when it comes to building meaningful connections in social situations. It can stem from a variety of causes, including past experiences, genetic predispositions, and societal pressures. One factor that may contribute to social anxiety is relationships. Whether it's the fear of rejection or the pressure to impress, navigating relationships can be daunting and overwhelming for some. In this article, we will explore how relationships may be contributing to social anxiety and isolation and provide tips for overcoming these challenges and building meaningful connections in social situations.

Understanding the Impact of Relationships on Social Anxiety:

Relationships, whether romantic or platonic, can have a significant impact on social anxiety. The fear of rejection, judgment, or abandonment can lead to a lack of confidence and a reluctance to engage in social situations. The pressure to impress or conform to certain societal expectations can also contribute to feelings of anxiety and isolation. These factors can make it difficult for individuals to form and maintain meaningful connections, leading to feelings of loneliness and isolation.

Tips for Overcoming Relationship-Induced Social Anxiety:

1. Practice Self-Compassion:

One of the most important steps in overcoming relationship-induced social anxiety is practicing self-compassion. This involves treating oneself with kindness, understanding, and acceptance, even in the face of perceived flaws or shortcomings. By acknowledging and accepting oneself, individuals can cultivate a sense of self-worth and confidence that can help alleviate social anxiety.

2. Challenge Negative Thought Patterns:

Negative thought patterns, such as assuming the worst or catastrophizing, can contribute to social anxiety. It is important to challenge these patterns and replace them with more balanced and realistic thoughts. This can involve questioning the evidence for negative beliefs and considering alternative perspectives.

3. Practice Mindfulness:

Practicing mindfulness, or being present in the moment without judgment, can help individuals reduce anxiety and increase their ability to engage in social situations. This can involve focusing on the present moment, observing one's thoughts and feelings without judgment, and using relaxation techniques such as deep breathing or meditation.

4. Seek Professional Help:

In some cases, relationship-induced social anxiety may require professional help. Therapy, such as cognitive-behavioral therapy, can help individuals identify and challenge negative thought patterns, develop social skills, and build self-confidence. Medication may also be prescribed in some cases to alleviate symptoms of anxiety.

5. Take Small Steps:

Overcoming relationship-induced social anxiety can be a gradual process. It is important to take small steps and gradually build up confidence and social skills. This can involve practicing social situations in a safe and controlled environment, such as with a trusted friend or family member, before gradually expanding to more challenging situations.

Overall, Relationships can play a significant role in social anxiety, but it is important to remember that these fears and anxieties can be overcome. By practicing self-compassion, challenging negative thought patterns, practicing mindfulness, seeking professional help, and taking small steps, individuals can build meaningful connections and overcome relationship-induced social anxiety.

In today's increasingly interconnected world, it is more important than ever to be able to build meaningful connections with people from diverse backgrounds and cultures. Whether you are working in a multicultural team, living in a diverse community, or simply looking to expand your social circle, being able to communicate effectively and bridge cultural gaps is essential.

One of the first steps in building connections across diverse communities is to approach others with an open mind and a willingness to learn. This means acknowledging and respecting differences in culture, beliefs, and values, and being open to learning about other people's perspectives and experiences. This can be done by actively seeking out opportunities to engage with people from different backgrounds, attending cultural events, or participating in intercultural programs.

Effective communication is also crucial in building connections across diverse communities. This includes not only verbal communication, but also nonverbal cues, body language, and tone of voice. It is important to be aware of your own communication style and how it may be perceived by others, as well as being receptive to feedback and willing to adapt your communication style to better connect with people from different cultures.

Another key strategy for building connections across diverse communities is to leverage technology to bridge communication and cultural gaps. This includes using translation apps to communicate with people who speak different languages, participating in online forums and social media groups that cater to diverse communities, and using virtual reality tools to experience different cultures and perspectives.

Building connections across diverse communities also requires a willingness to challenge your own assumptions and biases. This means being open to new experiences and perspectives, and recognizing and addressing your own biases and prejudices. It also means being willing to have difficult conversations about race, ethnicity, religion, and other cultural differences, and being willing to listen to and learn from other people's experiences.

In addition to the above strategies, it's important to recognize and respect the unique customs and traditions of diverse communities. This involves actively listening and learning about different cultural norms and values, as well as being open-minded and willing to adapt one's own behavior accordingly. By approaching interactions with empathy and a willingness to learn, individuals can build meaningful connections across diverse communities and foster a more inclusive and connected society.

Ultimately, building connections across diverse communities requires a commitment to empathy, understanding, and mutual respect. It is about recognizing and celebrating differences, while also finding common ground and shared values. With the right mindset and strategies in place, anyone can learn to build meaningful connections across diverse communities and cultures, and contribute to a more inclusive and connected world.

CONVINCING PEOPLE IN THE AGE OF AI

In the age of AI, the art of convincing people has taken on a new dimension. With the advent of AI-powered messaging and media, it has become increasingly difficult to connect with people and convince them of your viewpoint. To be persuasive in this era, you need to be able to cut through the noise and find ways to connect with your audience on a deeper level. In this chapter, we will explore some strategies for building persuasive arguments and communicating effectively in a world dominated by AI.

Understanding Your Audience:

The first step in convincing people in the age of AI is to understand your audience. You need to know what motivates them, what their values are, and what kind of messaging resonates with them. This requires a deep understanding of your target audience, which can be achieved through market research, data analysis, and social listening.

One of the key advantages of AI technology is that it can help you better understand your audience. By analyzing data from social media platforms, search engines, and other sources, AI algorithms can identify patterns in consumer behavior, sentiment, and preferences. This information can be used to tailor your messaging and create more persuasive arguments.

Building Trust:

Another important strategy for convincing people in the age of AI is to build trust. With so much misinformation and fake news circulating online, it's essential to establish yourself as a trustworthy source of information. This can be achieved through transparent communication, authentic messaging, and a consistent brand voice.

AI technology can also be used to build trust with your audience. For example, chatbots can be programmed to answer common questions and provide helpful information to customers. By providing accurate and timely responses, chatbots can help build trust and establish your brand as a reliable source of information.

Crafting Persuasive Arguments:

To be convincing in the age of AI, you need to be able to craft persuasive arguments. This requires a deep understanding of your audience, their needs, and their values. You also need to be able to present your arguments in a clear and concise manner, using language that resonates with your audience.

AI technology can be a valuable tool for crafting persuasive arguments. For example, natural language processing algorithms can analyze text to identify persuasive language patterns and suggest ways to improve your messaging. Similarly, machine learning algorithms can analyze data to identify patterns in consumer behavior and preferences, which can be used to craft more persuasive arguments.

Using AI to Connect with Your Audience:

Finally, AI technology can be used to connect with your audience in new and innovative ways. For example, chatbots can be programmed to engage with customers on social media platforms, providing personalized recommendations and answering common questions. Similarly, virtual assistants like Amazon's Alexa and Google Assistant can be used to deliver targeted messaging to consumers, based on their interests and preferences.

In conclusion, convincing people in the age of AI requires a deep understanding of your audience, their needs, and their values. It also requires a commitment to building trust and establishing yourself as a reliable source of information. With the right strategies and tools, however, it is possible to cut through the noise and connect with your audience on a deeper level. By leveraging AI technology, you can craft persuasive arguments, build trust, and connect with your audience in new and innovative ways.

CONCLUSION

In conclusion, building meaningful connections in the age of AI requires a combination of traditional social skills and an understanding of the technological tools available to us. AI technology can be a powerful aid in facilitating communication and understanding, but it cannot replace the importance of empathy, emotional intelligence, and active listening in building meaningful connections with others.

The strategies and tips discussed in this book aim to help individuals navigate the challenges of building connections in an increasingly technologically-driven world. By actively seeking out diverse communities, building empathy, and practicing effective communication, we can forge strong and authentic relationships with those around us.

It is important to recognize that building connections is a process that requires time, effort, and an openness to learning and growth. As AI continues to advance, we must continue to reflect on how it is impacting our social interactions and adapt our communication strategies accordingly.

Ultimately, the key to building meaningful connections in the age of AI is to approach technology as a tool to enhance, rather than replace, our human connection. By balancing our use of AI with traditional social skills, we can cultivate deeper and more authentic relationships, foster understanding and empathy, and create a more connected and harmonious world.

PART 3

DIGITAL COMMUNICATION ETIQUETTE

APPROPRIATE USE OF EMOJIS IN PROFESSIONAL COMMUNICATION

Emojis have become an integral part of digital communication, from personal messaging to professional emails. They allow people to convey emotions and add a touch of personality to their messages. However, when it comes to using emojis in professional communication, it's important to be cautious and thoughtful. In this article, we'll discuss the appropriate use of emojis in professional communication.

1. Know your audience: Understanding your audience is key to using emojis appropriately. If you're communicating with a colleague or client you've never met before, it's best to err on the side of caution and avoid using emojis until you've built a relationship.

2. Use emojis sparingly: Using too many emojis can be overwhelming and distracting. Stick to one or two emojis per message to avoid overwhelming your recipient.

3. Consider the context: Context is important when using emojis in professional communication. Make sure that the emoji you choose matches the tone and purpose of your message.

4. Don't use emojis in serious or negative situations: Avoid using emojis when delivering bad news or discussing serious topics. Emojis can be perceived as insensitive or unprofessional in these situations.

5. Choose appropriate emojis: Use emojis that are appropriate for professional communication. Avoid using overly expressive or suggestive emojis, and stick to ones that convey positive emotions such as gratitude, enthusiasm, or agreement.

6. Be consistent: If you choose to use emojis in your professional communication, be consistent in your use. Stick to the same emojis for similar messages to establish consistency and familiarity.

7. Avoid using emojis in subject lines: Using emojis in subject lines can make your email appear unprofessional and spammy. Stick to using them within the body of your message.

8. Use emojis to enhance, not replace, language: Emojis should enhance the message, not replace it. Use them to add emphasis or convey emotion, but don't rely on them to communicate your entire message.

9. Avoid using too many variations of the same emoji: Using too many variations of the same emoji can make your message difficult to read and understand. Stick to using one or two variations of the same emoji.

10. Don't overthink it: Emojis are meant to be fun and lighthearted. Don't overthink the use of emojis in professional communication, but make sure to use them appropriately and with consideration for your audience.

In summary, emojis can be a useful tool for conveying emotion and personality in professional communication, but it's important to use them thoughtfully and appropriately. Consider your audience, context, and message when deciding whether to use an emoji, and always aim to enhance, not detract from, your message.

APPROPRIATE USE OF EMOJIS IN PROFESSIONAL COMMUNICATION

Email communication is an essential part of professional communication, and it is crucial to know how to write an effective email to get your message across clearly. The way an email is written and structured can have a significant impact on how it is perceived by the recipient. Therefore, it is important to consider the addressing, tone, and structure of an email.

Addressing: The first thing to consider when writing an email is how to address the recipient. If you are emailing someone for the first time, it is best to use a formal greeting, such as "Dear Mr. Smith" or "Dear Dr. Johnson". If you have an ongoing professional relationship with the recipient, you may be able to use a more casual greeting, such as "Hi John" or "Hello Sarah". It is essential to ensure that you have the correct spelling of the recipient's name and the proper title.

Tone: The tone of an email can significantly impact how it is received by the recipient. You want to make sure that your tone is appropriate for the message you are trying to convey. If you are emailing a colleague or a business partner, it is best to use a professional tone that is friendly and respectful. Avoid using overly casual language, slang, or inappropriate humor. Additionally, it is important to be aware of the cultural norms and customs of the recipient's location, as what may be considered appropriate in one culture may not be in another.

Structure: The structure of an email can also have a significant impact on how it is received and understood by the recipient. It is essential to use proper formatting, including clear subject lines, salutations, and signatures. Additionally, it is essential to use short paragraphs, bullet points, and numbered lists to break up large blocks of text. This makes the email easier to read and understand, and it can also help ensure that the recipient reads the entire message.

In summary, proper email communication is critical for effective professional communication. When writing an email, it is essential to consider the addressing, tone, and structure of the email. By following these guidelines, you can ensure that your message is received positively and clearly understood by the recipient.

UNDERSTANDING TONE IN TEXT-BASED COMMUNICATION

Understanding tone in text-based communication has become increasingly important in today's digital world. With the rise of online messaging and email communication, it can be easy to misinterpret the tone of someone's message. It is essential to understand the nuances of text-based communication to avoid misunderstandings and ensure effective communication.

One of the biggest challenges of text-based communication is the absence of nonverbal cues, such as tone of voice, facial expressions, and body language. These nonverbal cues play a critical role in conveying tone and meaning in face-to-face conversations. However, in text-based communication, the tone can be easily misinterpreted. For example, a simple message like "fine" can be interpreted in many different ways, depending on the context and tone.

To understand the tone in text-based communication, it is essential to consider several factors. Firstly, it is important to pay attention to the language used in the message. Certain words and phrases may convey a particular tone, such as sarcasm or humor.

Secondly, the context of the message is crucial. A message sent in a formal work setting will likely have a different tone than a message sent to a friend.

Another important factor to consider is the relationship between the sender and the recipient. People have different communication styles, and knowing the other person's style can help in interpreting the tone. For example, if someone typically uses humor in their messages, it is more likely that a message with a joking tone is meant to be humorous.

One way to ensure effective communication in text-based communication is to use clear language and punctuation. The use of punctuation, such as exclamation marks, question marks, and ellipses, can help convey the intended tone of the message. For example, using an exclamation mark can help convey excitement or enthusiasm, while a question mark can indicate confusion or uncertainty.

It is also important to avoid making assumptions about the tone of the message. If you are unsure about the intended tone, it is better to ask the sender to clarify rather than making assumptions that can lead to misunderstandings.

In conclusion, understanding the tone in text-based communication is crucial to effective communication. It requires paying attention to the language used, context, relationship, and using clear language and punctuation. By being mindful of these factors, you can avoid misunderstandings and ensure that your message is received as intended.

UNDERSTANDING TONE IN TEXT-BASED COMMUNICATION

In today's digital age, most of our communication is text-based, whether it's email, instant messaging, or social media. One of the biggest challenges of text-based communication is understanding tone, which can often be misinterpreted or lost in translation. Understanding tone is crucial for effective communication, especially in professional settings where miscommunication can have serious consequences.

Here are some key aspects to consider when trying to understand tone in text-based communication:

1. Context: Understanding the context of the message is the first step in deciphering tone. Is it a casual conversation between friends or a professional email? The context will give you clues about the appropriate tone.

2. Word choice: The words that someone uses can convey a lot about their tone. Are they using formal language or colloquial expressions? Are they using positive or negative words?

3. Punctuation: Punctuation can make a big difference in the tone of a message. For example, a period can make a sentence sound more formal and serious, while an exclamation mark can make it sound more enthusiastic.

4. Emojis: Emojis are a popular way to convey tone in text-based communication. However, their meanings can be subjective and can vary across cultures and individuals. It's important to use them appropriately and in moderation.

5. Timing: The timing of a message can also impact its tone. For example, a message sent late at night may come across as more casual or informal than one sent during work hours.

6. Non-verbal cues: While text-based communication lacks the benefit of non-verbal cues like tone of voice and body language, there are still some non-verbal cues that can be used to convey tone. For example, using all caps or excessive punctuation can convey excitement or anger.

To effectively understand tone in text-based communication, it's important to read the message carefully and consider all of these factors. It's also important to ask for clarification if you're unsure about the tone of a message, especially in a professional setting.

By understanding tone, you can avoid misinterpretations and build stronger connections with others.

THE IMPORTANCE OF GRAMMAR AND SPELLING IN DIGITAL COMMUNICATION

In today's digital age, communication has become easier and more convenient than ever before. With just a few clicks or taps, we can send messages to anyone, anywhere in the world. However, the ease of digital communication can also lead to a lack of attention to detail, including grammar and spelling errors.

In digital communication, such as emails, text messages, and social media posts, it is important to pay attention to grammar and spelling. When we communicate with others, we want to ensure that our messages are clear and understandable. Grammatical errors can lead to confusion and misinterpretation, and spelling mistakes can make us look careless or uneducated.

Using proper grammar and spelling also shows that we value the recipient's time and effort. If we send a message that is riddled with errors, the recipient may have to spend extra time deciphering our message. This can be frustrating and can lead to a breakdown in communication.

Additionally, using proper grammar and spelling in digital communication can also enhance our professional image. Many employers and colleagues judge us based on the way we communicate, and using correct grammar and spelling can make us appear more professional and competent.

There are several ways to ensure that our digital communication is error-free. One way is to use spelling and grammar check tools that are built into many digital platforms, such as Microsoft Word and Gmail. These tools can help us catch mistakes before we hit the send button.

Another way to ensure proper grammar and spelling is to proofread our messages before sending them. Taking a few extra minutes to review our messages can help us catch errors that may have been missed by spell check tools.

In conclusion, proper grammar and spelling are important in all forms of communication, including digital communication. By paying attention to these details, we can ensure that our messages are clear, understandable, and reflect positively on our professional image.

EFFECTIVE USE OF SOCIAL MEDIA FOR PROFESSIONAL COMMUNICATION

Social media has become an essential tool for communication in today's society, with millions of people using it for personal and professional purposes. However, when it comes to using social media for professional communication, it's important to be aware of the best practices for effective and appropriate use.

Here are some tips for using social media for professional communication:

1. Choose the Right Platform: There are a variety of social media platforms available, each with their own strengths and weaknesses. It's important to choose the platform that is most appropriate for your professional needs. LinkedIn is often the go-to platform for professional networking, while Twitter and Instagram can be useful for sharing news and updates.

2. Create a Professional Profile: Your social media profile is often the first impression people will have of you, so it's important to create a professional and consistent image. Use a high-quality headshot for your profile picture and ensure your bio is clear and concise.

3. Be Mindful of Tone and Language: When communicating on social media, it's important to be mindful of your tone and language. Always use a professional tone, avoiding slang and jargon that may not be widely understood. Also, avoid using overly casual language or jokes that may not be appropriate in a professional context.

4. Share Valuable Content: One of the best ways to build your professional network on social media is by sharing valuable and relevant content. This could include articles, industry news, or your own insights on relevant topics. Sharing thoughtful and well-written content can help establish you as an expert in your field and attract other professionals to your profile.

5. Engage with Others: social media is a two-way street, so it's important to engage with others in your professional network. This could include commenting on other people's posts, sharing their content, or starting conversations on relevant topics. By engaging with others, you can build valuable relationships and establish yourself as a collaborative and supportive member of your professional community.

6. Respect Privacy and Confidentiality: When communicating on social media, it's important to respect the privacy and confidentiality of others. Never share confidential information or

personal details without permission, and be mindful of the privacy settings on your own social media accounts.

71

By following these tips, you can effectively use social media for professional communication and build meaningful connections with others in your industry. However, it's important to remember that social media is just one tool in your professional communication toolkit, and it should be used in conjunction with other forms of communication for a well-rounded and effective approach.

HANDLING COMMUNICATION IN GROUP CHATS: INCLUDING EVERYONE AND STAYING ON TOPIC

Group chats have become an integral part of modern communication, particularly in professional settings. However, managing group chats can be challenging, especially when it comes to ensuring that everyone is included and that the conversation stays on topic. In this section, we will discuss some strategies for handling communication in group chats effectively.

1. Establish clear guidelines: When you create a group chat, it is essential to establish clear guidelines from the beginning. This can include rules around the use of language, tone, and the topics that are appropriate for discussion. It is also a good idea to define the purpose of the group chat and who the intended audience is.

2. Keep the group chat focused: One of the biggest challenges in managing group chats is keeping the conversation focused on the intended topic. It is essential to ensure that everyone is clear on the purpose of the chat and that they stay on topic. You can achieve this by gently redirecting the conversation back to the topic whenever it begins to stray.

3. Ensure everyone is included: Group chats can be overwhelming, particularly for introverts or those who are not as comfortable in group settings. It is important to ensure that everyone has a chance to participate and that their contributions are valued. Encouraging everyone to speak up and sharing the airtime can help ensure that everyone feels included.

4. Avoid misunderstanding: In digital communication, misunderstandings can arise quickly. It is important to be clear in your communication, use appropriate language, and avoid jargon or slang that may be unfamiliar to some members of the group. It can also be helpful to use emojis or other visual aids to convey tone or emotion in your messages.

5. Use direct messages when necessary: Sometimes, a conversation may need to be taken offline or directed to a smaller group of people. In these situations, it is appropriate to use direct messages to communicate with specific individuals rather than involving the entire group.

6. Be respectful: Finally, it is crucial to be respectful in your communication with others in the group chat. This includes

avoiding personal attacks, name-calling, or other offensive language. Remember that everyone is entitled to their opinions and perspectives, and it is essential to create a safe and inclusive environment for everyone involved.

In conclusion, managing communication in group chats can be challenging, but with the right strategies, it can be done effectively. By establishing clear guidelines, keeping the conversation focused, ensuring everyone is included, avoiding misunderstandings, using direct messages when necessary, and being respectful, you can create a positive and productive environment for all members of the group.

USING APPROPRIATE LANGUAGE IN DIGITAL COMMUNICATION

Digital communication has become an essential part of our lives, and using appropriate language in such communication is crucial for maintaining a positive image and building strong relationships. The language used in digital communication is not limited to just words, but also includes tone, style, and context. In this section, we will discuss the importance of using appropriate language in digital communication and provide tips for effective communication.

Firstly, it is essential to understand that digital communication lacks the physical cues and context that we have in face-to-face communication. Therefore, we must use language that is clear, concise, and easily understandable. Ambiguity in digital communication can lead to misunderstandings and misinterpretations, which can harm relationships.

Secondly, it is essential to be mindful of the context in which we are communicating. For example, using casual language and abbreviations may be acceptable in personal communication with friends, but not in a professional setting. Similarly, using overly formal language may not be appropriate in casual communication.

Thirdly, it is important to use language that is inclusive and respectful. Avoid using language that could be considered offensive, discriminatory, or exclusionary. This includes avoiding derogatory language, slurs, or any language that may offend someone based on their gender, race, religion, or sexual orientation.

Fourthly, it is essential to be aware of the tone that we use in digital communication. Tone can be conveyed through the choice of words, the use of punctuation, and capitalization. For example, writing in all caps can convey anger or frustration, while using exclamation marks can convey excitement or enthusiasm. It is important to be mindful of the tone that we are using and ensure that it is appropriate for the context.

Finally, it is important to proofread our digital communication before sending it. Spelling mistakes, grammatical errors, and typos can make us appear unprofessional and careless. Therefore, it is crucial to double-check our communication before sending it.

In summary, using appropriate language in digital communication is crucial for building and maintaining strong relationships. It is important to use language that is clear, concise, and easily understandable, while being mindful of the context, tone, and inclusivity of our language. By following these tips, we can effectively communicate and build positive relationships in the digital world.

RESPONDING TO MESSAGES IN A TIMELY MANNER

Responding to messages in a timely manner is an important aspect of digital communication etiquette. With the prevalence of instant messaging and email, it is easy to let messages pile up and become overwhelming. However, it is essential to respond promptly to messages, especially those related to work or other important matters.

The first step in responding to messages in a timely manner is to set expectations for yourself and others. Let your contacts know when you are available and how quickly they can expect a response from you. For example, if you only check your email once a day, let your colleagues know that they can expect a response within 24 hours. If you are available to respond to instant messages during specific hours, make sure your contacts are aware of these hours.

Another strategy for responding to messages in a timely manner is to prioritize your messages. Start with the most urgent or important messages and work your way through the rest. This can help you stay focused and ensure that you are addressing the most pressing matters first.

It is also important to avoid procrastination when responding to messages. If you receive a message that requires a response, try to respond as soon as possible. This can prevent the message from getting lost in your inbox or being forgotten altogether. Even if you do not have time to fully address the message, a quick response to acknowledge receipt can go a long way in maintaining good communication with your contacts.

In addition to responding promptly, it is also important to be courteous and professional in your responses. Take the time to read and understand the message before responding, and avoid using overly casual or informal language. If you need more time to address a message or if you are unable to provide the requested information, communicate this clearly and professionally.

In summary, responding to messages in a timely manner is a key aspect of digital communication etiquette. Set expectations for yourself and others, prioritize your messages, avoid procrastination, and respond courteously and professionally. By following these guidelines, you can ensure that you are maintaining effective communication and building strong relationships with your contacts.

HANDLING CONFLICTS AND MISUNDERSTANDINGS IN DIGITAL COMMUNICATION

In today's world, digital communication is an essential part of our daily lives. Whether it is in the workplace, with friends, or family, we rely heavily on digital communication to connect with others. While digital communication can be convenient and efficient, it can also lead to misunderstandings and conflicts, especially when messages are misinterpreted or tone is unclear. In this context, it is important to know how to handle conflicts and misunderstandings in digital communication.

The first step in handling conflicts and misunderstandings is to identify the problem. Misunderstandings can arise from a variety of sources, including ambiguous language, cultural differences, and emotional triggers. Once the problem has been identified, it is important to address it directly and calmly. This means avoiding the temptation to escalate the situation by responding with anger or frustration.

In many cases, misunderstandings can be resolved through open communication. It may be helpful to clarify the message or ask for clarification. This can help to prevent misinterpretation and ensure that both parties are on the same page. It is also important to acknowledge the other person's perspective and feelings. This can help to defuse the situation and create a more positive atmosphere for resolving the conflict.

When conflicts cannot be resolved through open communication, it may be necessary to seek the help of a third party. This could be a manager or supervisor in a workplace setting or a mediator in a personal setting. Third parties can help to facilitate communication and find a solution that is acceptable to both parties.

Prevention is also key to avoiding conflicts and misunderstandings in digital communication. This includes setting clear expectations for communication, using appropriate language and tone, and avoiding emotionally charged messages. It is also important to be mindful of cultural differences and to consider the impact of language on others.

In conclusion, digital communication can be a powerful tool for connecting with others, but it can also lead to conflicts and misunderstandings. By being aware of the potential for misinterpretation and taking steps to prevent and resolve conflicts, we can create more positive and productive relationships in the digital world.

RESPECTING OTHERS' PRIVACY AND BOUNDARIES IN DIGITAL COMMUNICATION

Respecting others' privacy and boundaries in digital communication is an essential aspect of building and maintaining healthy relationships in the online world. With the growing use of digital communication platforms, it is important to understand and implement respectful communication practices to avoid misunderstandings and conflicts.

One of the most important principles of respecting others' privacy and boundaries in digital communication is to obtain consent before sharing personal information or images. This means asking for permission before sharing someone else's photo, video, or other personal information. Even if the information seems harmless or is widely known, it is important to respect the other person's right to control their own information.

Another key principle is to respect people's time and availability. In digital communication, it is easy to assume that others are always available and willing to engage in conversation, but this is not always the case. It is important to ask if the person has time to talk or respond to messages before expecting an immediate response.

In addition, it is important to set and respect boundaries around communication. This includes not bombarding someone with messages or constantly demanding their attention. If someone expresses that they need space or time to themselves, it is important to respect their wishes and avoid contacting them until they are ready.

Another important aspect of respecting others' privacy and boundaries in digital communication is to be mindful of the content and tone of messages. Avoid making assumptions or passing judgment based on someone's online activity or behavior. Similarly, avoid using language that is disrespectful, hurtful, or offensive, even if it is meant as a joke.

When conflicts or misunderstandings do arise, it is important to address them respectfully and directly. Avoid resorting to passive-aggressive behavior or gossiping with others about the issue. Instead, express your concerns or feelings in a clear and respectful manner, and be open to hearing the other person's perspective.

Overall, respecting others' privacy and boundaries in digital communication requires thoughtful consideration of others' feelings, time, and autonomy. By following these principles, we can build and maintain healthy and respectful relationships in the digital world.

PART 4

SPECIAL AI TOOL

HUMAN PSYCHOLOGY MEETS INTELLIGENT AUTOMATION

"IMAGINEX": THE AI-POWERED MESSAGING APP FOR ENHANCED PROFESSIONAL COMMUNICATION

ImagineX, the messaging app with AI-powered users, can significantly help in building relationships. With the app's incorporation of AI technology, it can provide personalized and creative solutions to various tasks in different fields, making communication more efficient and effective.

The use of AI-powered users in the app can enhance group communication, planning, and visualization, making it easier for users to collaborate and achieve their goals. For instance, in the travel example, AI-powered users GenieX and PicassoX provided suggestions and generated images that helped the group finalize their itinerary, resulting in a successful trip. In the fashion example, GenieX and PicassoX helped the group select their outfits and accessories, resulting in a stunning appearance at the wedding. In the food example, GenieX and PicassoX helped the group prepare delicious food and have a successful party.

With ImagineX, users can improve their communication and collaboration skills, which are crucial in building strong relationships. By working together in a group and utilizing the app's AI-powered users, users can achieve their goals efficiently and creatively. Moreover, the app's personalized responses and services can help users feel more connected and valued, ultimately strengthening relationships.

As the author of " HUMAN PSYCHOLOGY MEETS INTELLIGENT AUTOMATION : The brainf*cking Guide for Building Relations," I have created ImagineX to help people in their communication and collaboration needs. I believe that by incorporating AI technology into messaging apps, we can provide more efficient and effective solutions to tasks, resulting in better relationships and overall well-being. If you would like to access ImagineX, please feel free to request me on LinkedIn.

PART 5

CONSPIRACY THEORIES

WORKPLACE CONSPIRACY

A workplace conspiracy occurs when a group of colleagues or even management conspire against an individual to undermine their career, reputation, or both. It can manifest in various ways, such as spreading rumors, withholding information or opportunities, sabotaging work, or deliberately creating conflicts. If left unchecked, a workplace conspiracy can cause immense stress, anxiety, and even damage to an individual's mental health and professional life. Here are some steps that an individual can take to tackle a situation of workplace conspiracy:

1. Document everything: It is important to document any evidence that may support your claims of a workplace conspiracy. This can include emails, text messages, meeting notes, performance reviews, and any other relevant documentation. Having evidence to back up your claims can strengthen your case and make it easier to prove any wrongdoing.

2. Speak to a trusted colleague: It can be helpful to speak to a colleague you trust about your concerns. They may be able to provide insight into the situation or even help you gather

evidence. However, be sure to choose someone who is trustworthy and discreet.

3. Talk to a manager or HR: If the conspiracy involves management or is too serious to handle alone, consider speaking to a manager or HR representative. They can investigate the situation and take appropriate action if necessary.

4. Keep a level head: It's important to remain calm and composed when dealing with a workplace conspiracy. Reacting emotionally or aggressively may make the situation worse. Instead, try to remain professional and focus on finding a resolution.

5. Build strong relationships: Building strong relationships with coworkers can help prevent workplace conspiracies from happening in the first place. It's important to be a team player, offer support and encouragement, and avoid gossip and drama.

6. Focus on your work: Despite the conspiracy, it's important to stay focused on your work and continue performing at a high

level. This can help prove your worth to the company and demonstrate your professionalism.

7. Consider legal action: In extreme cases, it may be necessary to consider legal action. If you believe that you have been a victim of workplace discrimination or harassment, consider consulting with a lawyer to discuss your legal options.

In conclusion, workplace conspiracies can be damaging and stressful, but there are steps that an individual can take to tackle the situation. By documenting everything, speaking to trusted colleagues or management, remaining professional, and building strong relationships, an individual can minimize the impact of a workplace conspiracy and even come out on top.

RELATIONSHIP CONSPIRACY

A relationship conspiracy can be a challenging situation to handle, especially when the person trying to undermine your relationship is someone close to you. Here are some steps that you can take to tackle a situation of relationship conspiracy:

1. Identify the conspirator: The first step in handling a relationship conspiracy is to identify the person who is trying to undermine your relationship. It could be a friend, family member, or even your partner's ex. Once you have identified the person, it will be easier to address the situation.

2. Talk to your partner: Open and honest communication is key in any relationship. Discuss with your partner about what is happening and how it is affecting you. Make sure to express your concerns without blaming your partner.

3. Set boundaries: If the conspirator is someone you know, it is essential to set boundaries with them. Let them know that their behavior is not acceptable and that it is affecting your relationship. You may need to limit your interactions with them or cut them out of your life entirely.

4. Seek professional help: If you are finding it difficult to handle the situation on your own, seeking professional help can be beneficial. A therapist can help you work through your emotions and develop strategies to tackle the situation effectively.

5　Strengthen your relationship: Work on strengthening your relationship with your partner. Spend quality time together, communicate openly, and show each other love and support. A strong relationship can withstand any outside interference.

6.　Stay positive: Finally, it's essential to maintain a positive outlook and not let the conspiracy affect your mental health. Surround yourself with people who love and support you, engage in activities that make you happy, and focus on the positive aspects of your relationship.

In summary, tackling a relationship conspiracy requires identifying the conspirator, communicating openly with your partner, setting boundaries, seeking professional help if necessary, strengthening your relationship, and staying positive. Remember, a strong and healthy relationship can withstand any outside interference.

FAMILY CONSPIRACY

A family conspiracy can be a particularly painful and difficult situation to deal with, as it involves betrayal and manipulation from those who are closest to us. Here are some steps that can help a person tackle a situation of family conspiracy:

1. Identify the source of the conspiracy: Try to understand who is behind the conspiracy and why they are targeting you. This will help you determine the best course of action.

2. Maintain your composure: It is important to remain calm and composed when dealing with a family conspiracy. Avoid reacting in anger or frustration, as this can exacerbate the situation.

3. Seek support: Reach out to other family members or close friends who can offer emotional support and help you navigate the situation.

4. Communicate directly: If possible, try to address the situation directly with the family member(s) involved. Explain how their actions are affecting you and try to find a resolution.

5. Set boundaries: If the family member(s) continue to conspire against you, it may be necessary to set boundaries to protect yourself. This could involve limiting contact or cutting ties altogether.

6. Seek professional help: If the situation becomes overwhelming, consider seeking the help of a therapist or counselor. They can provide valuable guidance and support as you navigate the difficult emotions and dynamics involved in a family conspiracy.

7. Document everything: If the conspiracy involves illegal or unethical behavior, it is important to document any evidence that may be useful in legal proceedings.

Dealing with a family conspiracy can be an emotionally draining and challenging experience. However, by remaining calm, seeking support, and taking proactive steps to protect yourself, you can overcome the situation and move forward with your life.

ROMANTIC CONSPIRACY

Dealing with a romantic conspiracy can be tricky and emotionally draining. Here are some tips to help you tackle the situation:

1. Communicate openly with your partner: Be open and honest with your partner about what is going on. Discuss your concerns and how the conspiracy is affecting your relationship. Communication is key to building a strong and trusting relationship.

2. Identify the source of the conspiracy: Try to find out who is behind the conspiracy and why they are doing it. Is it an ex-partner who is jealous? A friend who is trying to come between you and your partner? Knowing the source of the conspiracy can help you develop a plan to counter it.

3. Don't react impulsively: It can be tempting to react impulsively and lash out at the person behind the conspiracy. However, this can make the situation worse and damage your relationship further. Stay calm and think carefully about your actions.

4. Set boundaries: If someone is trying to come between you and your partner, it's important to set boundaries. Make it clear to them that their behavior is not acceptable and that you will not tolerate it.

7. Get support: Dealing with a romantic conspiracy can be emotionally draining. It's important to have a support system in place. Reach out to friends and family members for support. Consider seeing a therapist or counselor who can help you work through your feelings.

6. Focus on your relationship: Don't let the conspiracy consume your relationship. Instead, focus on building a strong and healthy relationship with your partner. Spend time together and make an effort to show your love and appreciation for each other.

7. Take legal action if necessary: If the conspiracy involves illegal activity, such as stalking or harassment, consider taking legal action. Consult with a lawyer to explore your options.

Dealing with a romantic conspiracy can be difficult, but it's important to remember that you are not alone. By communicating openly with your partner, identifying the source of the conspiracy, setting boundaries, and getting support, you can overcome the situation and strengthen your relationship.

ACADEMIC CONSPIRACY

Dealing with an academic conspiracy can be a challenging and frustrating experience. However, there are several steps that a person can take to tackle such a situation:

1. Document everything: Keep a record of all the interactions and conversations related to the conspiracy. This includes emails, text messages, and other forms of communication.

2. Identify the source of the conspiracy: Try to identify who is behind the conspiracy and why they are doing it. This will help in formulating an effective strategy to deal with the situation.

3. Talk to a trusted advisor: Speak to a trusted professor or mentor in the academic community who can provide guidance and support.

4. Seek legal advice: If the conspiracy involves criminal activity such as plagiarism or fraud, seek legal advice and consider taking legal action.

5. Build a support network: Reach out to colleagues, friends, and family for emotional support. Dealing with a conspiracy can be stressful and overwhelming, having a support network can make it easier to cope.

6. Remain professional: Do not let the conspiracy affect your work or academic performance. Continue to focus on your goals and strive for excellence.

7. Address the issue directly: Confront the individual or individuals involved in the conspiracy in a professional and respectful manner. Explain the impact of their actions and try to find a resolution.

Dealing with an academic conspiracy can be a complex and difficult situation. It is important to remain calm, professional, and seek support from trusted advisors and colleagues. By taking the necessary steps, it is possible to overcome the situation and continue to achieve academic success.

FINANCIAL CONSPIRACY

Dealing with a financial conspiracy can be a daunting task, especially if the perpetrator has a significant financial advantage over you. However, there are a few steps you can take to protect yourself and potentially recover any losses.

1. Document everything: Keep a record of all financial transactions, communications, and agreements. This documentation can serve as evidence in case of legal action.

2. Seek legal advice: Consult a lawyer who specializes in financial disputes. They can advise you on the legal options available and help you build a case against the perpetrator.

3. Check your financial accounts: Regularly check your bank accounts, credit card statements, and other financial records for any unauthorized transactions or suspicious activity. If you notice any discrepancies, report them to the financial institution immediately.

4. Hire a financial advisor: Consider hiring a financial advisor to help you manage your assets and investments. They can provide you with unbiased advice and help you make informed financial decisions.

5. Build a support network: Reach out to friends, family, and colleagues for emotional support during this difficult time. Additionally, consider joining a support group for individuals who have experienced financial abuse or fraud.

6. Stay vigilant: Be cautious when sharing financial information and be on the lookout for any suspicious activity or behavior from the perpetrator.

7. Take care of yourself: The stress of dealing with a financial conspiracy can take a toll on your mental and physical health. Make sure to prioritize self-care and seek professional help if necessary.

It is essential to take swift action to protect yourself and your financial assets when dealing with a financial conspiracy. Seeking legal and financial advice and building a support network can help you navigate the situation and potentially recover any losses.

SOCIETAL CONSPIRACY

Dealing with a societal conspiracy can be particularly challenging because it often involves deeply ingrained societal beliefs and structures that can be difficult to change. Here are some steps you can take to tackle a situation of a societal conspiracy:

1. Recognize and acknowledge the issue: The first step is to recognize that there is a societal conspiracy at play and acknowledge the harm it is causing you. This can involve educating yourself about the issue and seeking support from individuals or groups who are working towards addressing it.

2. Speak out: Speaking out about the issue can be a powerful way to raise awareness and encourage change. This can involve talking to individuals, sharing your story on social media, or joining protests or rallies.

3. Build alliances: Building alliances with individuals or groups who share your beliefs and values can be a powerful way to amplify your message and build momentum for change.

4. Take legal action: In some cases, legal action may be necessary to address the harm caused by a societal conspiracy. This can involve filing a complaint with a government agency, working with a lawyer to file a lawsuit, or advocating for policy change at the local or national level.

5. Practice self-care: Dealing with a societal conspiracy can be emotionally and mentally draining, so it's important to prioritize self-care. This can involve seeking therapy, spending time with supportive friends and family, or engaging in activities that bring you joy and help you recharge.

It's important to remember that tackling a societal conspiracy can be a long and difficult journey, but by taking action and standing up for what you believe in, you can help create positive change for yourself and others.

CELEBRITY CONSPIRACY

Dealing with a celebrity conspiracy can be particularly challenging because of the high level of attention and scrutiny that comes with being a public figure. Here are some steps that can be taken to tackle this situation:

1. Stay calm: It's important to remain calm and not react impulsively to any rumors or conspiracies. Responding in a defensive or aggressive manner may only make the situation worse.

2. Gather evidence: Collect evidence that disproves any false claims or rumors. This could include documentation, witnesses, or even social media posts.

3. Engage with fans and supporters: Engage with fans and supporters who are spreading positive messages about

you. This can help counter any negative messages that are being spread.

4. Speak out: Consider speaking out publicly about the situation. This could involve issuing a statement or giving an interview to a reputable media outlet.

5. Seek legal advice: If the situation has resulted in legal implications, seek the advice of a legal professional to explore your options and ensure that your rights are protected.

6. Keep a positive attitude: Maintain a positive attitude and focus on your work or personal life outside of the situation. Remember that the conspiracy will eventually fade away, and your positive actions will speak for themselves.

BUSINESS CONSPIRACY

A business conspiracy can be a serious threat to your career or business. Here are some steps you can take to tackle this situation:

1. Gather evidence: The first step in tackling a business conspiracy is to gather evidence of any wrongdoing. This may include emails, messages, and other documentation that shows the conspiracy in action.

2. Seek legal advice: Once you have evidence of the conspiracy, seek legal advice from a qualified lawyer. They can advise you on your legal rights and help you develop a strategy for dealing with the conspiracy.

3. Be proactive: Don't wait for the conspiracy to harm your business or career. Be proactive and take steps to protect your assets, clients, and reputation. This may involve hiring a public

relations firm to manage your image and communicate with the
public.

4. Build alliances: Business conspiracies can be difficult to fight
alone. Build alliances with other people in your industry or
community who can help you fight the conspiracy. This may
include other business owners, professional organizations, or
industry groups.

5. Stay focused: It's important to stay focused on your business
goals and not get distracted by the conspiracy. Focus on delivering
high-quality products or services and building strong relationships
with your clients. This will help you weather any storm created by
the conspiracy.

Maintain your integrity: Above all, maintain your integrity and
reputation. Don't stoop to the level of the conspirators by
engaging in unethical or illegal behavior. Stick to your values and
principles, and let the truth speak for itself.

SOCIAL MEDIA CONSPIRACY

Dealing with a social media conspiracy can be challenging, but it is important to take action to protect your online reputation. Here are some steps you can take:

1. Document everything: Take screenshots of any posts, comments, or messages that are harmful to your reputation. Keep track of who is involved and what they are saying.

2. Respond appropriately: It can be tempting to respond with anger or defensiveness, but this can often make the situation worse. Instead, respond calmly and professionally. Address any false statements with facts and evidence.

3. Report the harassment: Most social media platforms have policies against harassment and hate speech. Report any abusive behavior to the platform's moderators.

4. Reach out for support: Don't try to handle the situation alone. Reach out to trusted friends or family members for emotional support, or consider seeking the help of a professional counselor.

5. Consider legal action: In some cases, legal action may be necessary. If you are being targeted by false accusations or libelous statements, you may want to consult with a lawyer to explore your options.

Overall, the key to dealing with a social media conspiracy is to stay calm, document everything, and take appropriate action to protect your reputation. Remember that your online reputation is an important part of your personal and professional life, and it is worth taking steps to safeguard it.

WRAP UP

CONCLUSION

In conclusion, "Human Psychology Meets Intelligent Automation " is a book that is relevant to people from all walks of life, regardless of their level of familiarity with technology. In this book, we explored how the intersection of human psychology and artificial intelligence is shaping the way we live, work, and communicate.

Through this book, you learned about strategies to help you navigate the complex world of technology, as well as the importance of digital etiquette in our increasingly connected world. You gained insight into how AI is changing the way we approach problem-solving and decision-making, and how it is transforming industries ranging from healthcare to finance.

Whether you are a business owner seeking to optimize your operations with AI or an individual looking to improve your digital literacy skills, "Human Psychology Meets Intelligent Automation " has something for everyone. We hope that this book has broadened your understanding of the ways in which AI is transforming our lives, and has given you the tools to thrive in the digital age.

Ultimately , by taking a thoughtful and strategic approach to AI, we can harness its full potential and create a brighter future for ourselves and future generations.

ACKNOWLEDGEMENT

I would like to express my heartfelt gratitude to everyone who has supported me throughout the writing of this book.

Firstly, I would like to thank my family for their unwavering support and encouragement. They have been my biggest cheerleaders and have provided me with the motivation and inspiration I needed to see this project through to completion.

I would also like to extend my thanks to my friends and colleagues who have provided me with invaluable feedback and insights throughout the writing process. Their constructive criticism and encouragement have been instrumental in helping me refine my ideas and improve the quality of this book.

I am also grateful to the experts in the field of human psychology and artificial intelligence who generously shared their knowledge and expertise with me. Their insights and perspectives have enriched this book and helped me to create a work that is both informative and engaging.

Lastly, I would like to express my gratitude to the readers who will take the time to read this book. Your interest and support are greatly appreciated, and I hope that this work will provide you with valuable insights and perspectives on the intersection of human psychology and AI.

SHORT NOTE BY AUTHOR

Dear readers,

I am humbled and grateful for your interest in my book "Human Psychology Meets AI". It has been a privilege to share my thoughts and insights with you, and I hope that this book has been informative and thought-provoking.

As we continue to navigate a world that is increasingly shaped by technology, I believe it is more important than ever to understand the impact that it has on our lives, both personally and professionally. By exploring the intersection of human psychology and artificial intelligence, I hope to have provided you with a greater understanding of the ways in which these two fields can intersect and influence each other.

Thank you for taking the time to read my book, and I look forward to hearing your feedback and thoughts on how we can continue to explore and shape the future of technology together.

Best regards,

Gurnain Singh Wadhwa

COPYRIGHT

HOW TO REACH AUTHOR

LinkedIn- https://www.linkedin.com/in/gurnainwadhwa

Portfolio- https://gurnainwadhwa.netlify.app/

Mail-   gurnainwadhwa2505@gmail.com